Water Crisis

Edited by Jessica Cohn

www.av2books.com

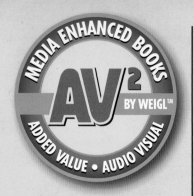

AV² provides enriched content that supplements and complements this book. Weigl's AV² books strive to create inspired learning and engage young minds in a total learning experience.

Your AV² Media Enhanced books come alive with...

Audio
Listen to sections of the book read aloud.

Key Words
Study vocabulary, and complete a matching word activity.

Video
Watch informative video clips.

Quizzes
Test your knowledge.

Embedded Weblinks
Gain additional information for research.

Slide Show
View images and captions, and prepare a presentation.

Try This!
Complete activities and hands-on experiments.

... and much, much more!

Go to **www.av2books.com**, and enter this book's unique code.

BOOK CODE

J316648

AV² by Weigl brings you media enhanced books that support active learning.

Download the AV² catalog at
www.av2books.com/catalog

AV² Online Navigation on page 48

Published by AV² by Weigl
350 5ᵗʰ Avenue, 59ᵗʰ Floor
New York, NY 10118

Website: www.av2books.com   www.weigl.com

Library of Congress Control Number: 2013941894

ISBN 978-1-62127-441-4 (hardcover)
ISBN 978-1-62127-447-6 (softcover)
ISBN 978-1-62127-837-5 (single-user eBook)
ISBN 978-1-48961-724-8 (multi-user eBook)

Printed in the United States of America in North Mankato, Minnesota
1 2 3 4 5 6 7 8 9 0 17 16 15 14 13

062013
WEP220513

Weigl acknowledges Getty Images as its primary image supplier for this title.

Every reasonable effort has been made to trace ownership and to obtain permission to reprint copyright material. The publishers would be pleased to have any errors or omissions brought to their attention so that they may be corrected in subsequent printings.

Project Coordinator: Aaron Carr
Art Director: Terry Paulhus

Water Crisis

CONTENTS

Introduction to the Water Crisis

Seventy-one percent of the surface of Earth is covered by water. Yet, each day people around the world suffer from a lack of water. Most of the water that exists on Earth is seawater. Less than 3 percent of the world's water supply is **fresh water**, and less than half of this is usable. Freshwater resources are not evenly distributed among the nations of the world. Canada, for example, has one-fifth of the world's fresh water. Most of the other nations do not have enough water to meet their needs.

Importance of Water

"The World Health Organization says that by the year 2025, it is likely that two out of three people will be living in stressful water conditions."

Uses of Water

"Improvements in **irrigation** would reduce waste and make an important difference in relieving the strain on the supply of fresh water."

Loss of Water

Protection of Water

"Cleaning up the water that has been polluted is a major issue, especially when underground water is involved."

"With education, everyone can make better decisions about water projects and learn to conserve and build upon the supply of fresh water."

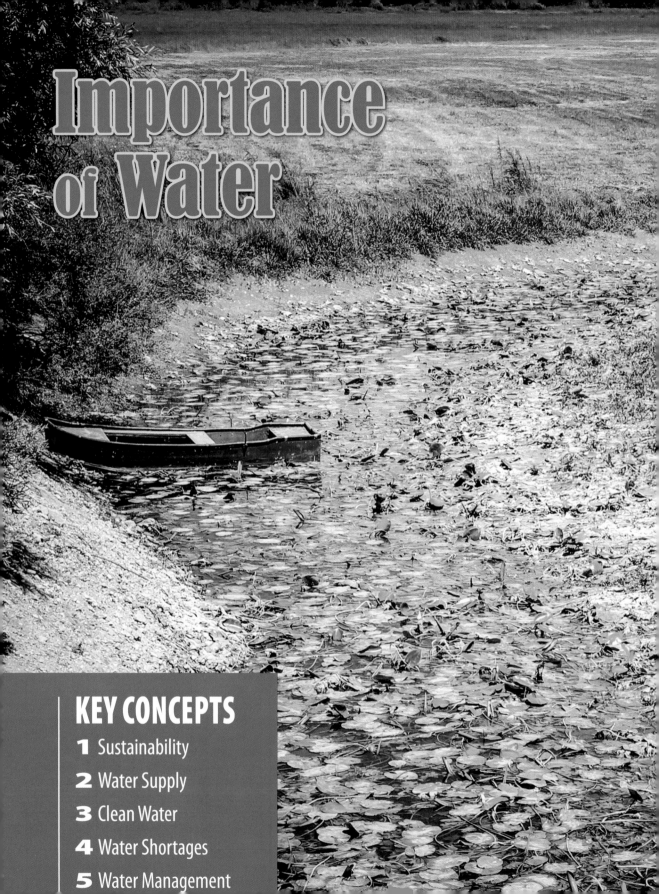

Importance of Water

Now more than ever, the management of the world's water resources is an issue that demands attention. A reliable water supply is essential to support life on Earth. The supply and use of water vary greatly from one area to another. Yet, officials in every region are now facing the challenge of making sure there is enough good-quality water for the people who need it.

1 Sustainability

Sustainability is the ability to use resources so that they are not used up or damaged. Only if fresh water is used in a sustainable way will it be able to meet the needs of people around the world. Sustainability is also important to ensure that good-quality water is available for people in the future.

In some parts of the world, water sustainability is especially difficult. People in some regions depend on monsoons for water. A monsoon is a seasonal wind that can bring heavy rainfall. Monsoons do not come every year, so the rainwater must be saved. Yet, in some years, there can be so much rain that it causes flooding.

People in the **developed world** often take water for granted, but around the world, clean water is a precious resource. It is common for people in developed nations to use more than 110 gallons (415 liters) of water each day. Elsewhere, many people get by on barely 2.2 gallons (8.3 L) of water on a daily basis. Millions of people go without enough water.

According to the **United Nations (UN)**, more than 780 million people around the world do not have clean water for drinking, cooking, or bathing. Two out of five people in the world live in unsanitary, or dirty, conditions. They do not have toilets or sewers to remove their waste.

Wars and other international problems also affect the sustainability of the water supply. Some areas may have more water than they need, but it is difficult and expensive to move water long distances to places where there is a shortage. Managing the world's water supply means dealing with many challenges.

In 2013, about half of U.S. states experienced unusually long periods without rain, according to the federal government.

A lake near Indianapolis, Indiana, dried up in 2012. That summer, more than 1,000 counties across 26 U.S. states were declared natural disaster areas.

2 Water Supply

People in the developed world have become used to the idea that water is cheap and plentiful. The average citizen in the United States uses about 150 gallons (570 L) of water each day. This includes water for drinking, cooking, bathing, and **sanitation**. By contrast, each person in Africa south of the Sahara Desert uses just 2.6 to 5.2 gallons (10 to 20 L) per day.

As countries become more developed, their citizens use more water. The demand for water rises as their people enjoy a better **standard of living**. In addition, the number of people is rising across the globe. For both of these reasons, there has been a steady rise in water use. Together, a larger global population and an increase in the amount of water used per person puts stress on the world's supply of fresh water.

Some sources of water are **renewable**, but many are not. Libya, for example, pumps water from ancient aquifers, which are underground areas of water-filled rock. At the rate Libya now uses water, this source will empty in 50 to 100 years. Saudi Arabia grows wheat in the desert using water from underground aquifers. These aquifers will never be refilled with water because there is almost no rain in Saudi Arabia.

In the United States, the massive Ogallala aquifer lies in the Great Plains between South Dakota and northwest Texas. At least one-quarter of that reserve of water has been pumped from the ground. In Mexico, **water tables** are dropping very quickly in the capital, Mexico City. The cities of Beijing in China, Bangkok in Thailand, and other major population centers around the world face a similar problem.

Does Underground Water Belong to the People Who Own Property Above It?

People who buy land pay for the right to use the surface of the land as they see fit. This is true as long as the landowners follow the customs and laws that have to do with their property. Various laws are in force in order to protect others who may be affected by the actions of the property owners.

The question is, do landowners also own special rights to any underground water that their property sits above? In many areas of the world, the **groundwater** is valuable and becoming even more so. In some places, people are pumping more water from the ground than can be replaced, so the water is in danger of being used up.

Property Owners
Yes, the water belongs to the property owners. The aquifers under our land support our farms and ranches. The water supply is part of our property, and we should be able to use it and even sell it to others.

Local and State Officials
Growing cities require more and more water to sustain the numbers of people living there. The water in any given area belongs to its **municipalities** and states, not just to property owners.

Federal Officials
In many cases, a large number of municipalities draw from the same aquifer, but some take more water than others. The water supply is a resource that national government should be overseeing.

Water Activists
The water supply belongs to everyone on the planet. Water is being used at a faster rate than it is being replaced. We need new laws to regulate the use of water for the benefit of all the people around the world.

For   Supportive   Undecided   Unsupportive   Against

3 Clean Water

People with easy access to clean water may not be concerned with the water supply because they do not think it is a serious problem. In truth, however, the supply is limited. Only a small percentage of the world's water is suitable for drinking, farming, or industry. To complicate matters, most of the water is not actually available. About 70 percent of fresh water is either frozen in ice around Earth's poles or located deep in the ground.

In addition, the term *fresh water* can be misleading. Not all fresh water is clean enough to drink. Most of the rivers and lakes in the world are polluted. In fact, many species of plants and animals that live in rivers and lakes are struggling to stay healthy. Some of these species are in danger of becoming **extinct**. At one lake in the country of Turkey, at least 12 species of fish have died out in recent years.

Dirty water is a danger to humans as well. Polluted water may contain disease-causing parasites, which are tiny creatures that live on or with other living beings. Diseases carried by water are major causes of death in the **developing world**. Each day, millions of people are at risk because they do not have access to clean water.

Giardiasis is one of the most common diseases carried by water. People can get this disease when they contact water contaminated with feces. Dirty water can carry the giardiasis parasite into human intestines, where these parasites like to live.

Dirty water carries many different types of bacteria and viruses. Shigella is a type of water-carried bacteria that causes diarrhea, fever, and stomach cramps. People with cholera, which is also caused by bacteria found in water, can die within hours due to diarrhea and rapid loss of fluids.

Just living near dirty water can be deadly. Each year, more than a million people die from malaria. This disease is caused by parasites. They are carried to people through mosquito bites. Mosquitoes breed in still water, both dirty and clean, but the disease is most common in poor areas, where the water supply and sanitation are limited.

A large canal serving Lahore, Pakistan, has been polluted by sewage and industrial waste.

4 Water Shortages

For anyone used to seeing water flow from faucets, it can be hard to believe that there is not enough water to meet everyone's needs. Think of all the times that people in the developed world use or come in contact with water throughout each day. Each morning, millions of people brush their teeth and take showers. They wash fruit and fill pots with water for cooking. They water plants and take long drinks of water after exercising.

Many people in the developed world waste water. Individuals allow their showers to run longer than needed. People discard water that could be used to water plants or clean outdoor items. In addition, businesses and governments do not always do a good job in managing their water supplies. The water used in industries and on farms can become polluted with chemicals, which further reduces the water supply.

People in developed countries are often unaware of water shortages in other parts of the world. Many people feel too busy to think about the needs of people in other countries. Yet, the water shortage problem is growing worldwide.

About 40 percent of the world's population is already experiencing water shortages. These people live in 80 different countries. The World Health Organization says that by the year 2025, it is likely that two out of three people worldwide will be living in stressful water conditions.

In Japan, about 70 percent of drinking water comes from rivers and streams. Much of Japan's water comes from monsoons, which feed the rivers.

5 Water Management

Water management is the planning and distribution of water resources. Water managers first consider the needs of the people who benefit from a specific source of water. Then, they must think about needs across the globe. Water cannot be created, so it has to be shared. The world's fresh water is a resource that has to be handled with care.

Knowing the facts is the first step of water management. Earth's supply of water is the same now as it was 1 million years ago. Yet, the number of people has multiplied a great deal over that same time period. Today, there are more people to feed, and more water is needed to raise crops. Meanwhile, a great deal of the water sent to farms is wasted. About 60 percent of water that flows to farms is not really needed for the plants to grow.

Many developing regions of the world lack the tools and technology to move water from one place to another. To deliver clean water to areas that need it, major **dams**, **pipelines**, and **aqueduct** systems can be built. These systems can store large volumes of fresh water and transfer it to other locations. These facilities, however, are very costly. Often, they have a negative effect on the environment.

In addition, water is different from resources and products such as fuel, minerals, or manufactured goods. Unlike gasoline, cars, and other goods, water is not often shipped from one continent to another. This cannot be done easily. Major water projects often end up helping the people in just one region.

Sources of Fresh Water

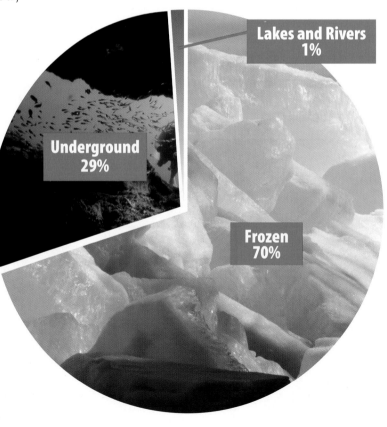

Lakes and Rivers 1%

Underground 29%

Frozen 70%

Will Water Scarcity Around the World Lead to War?

Much of the world's population lives near rivers. Many of these rivers are shared by more than one country. In Europe, for example, there are about 175 agreements governing how various countries will share water. In other parts of the world, where many countries do not have agreements with their neighbors, no one is certain who controls or "owns" the water.

When water flows across international borders, it is hard to determine which country owns the water. Sometimes, countries reach agreements on how to share water, but when they do not, conflicts can develop.

United Nations
Yes, water scarcity might lead to war. Our studies show that 30 nations will be "water scarce" by the year 2025. The UN Security Council needs to work out ways to encourage cooperation over water before it is too late.

World Bank
Our experts at the **World Bank** estimate that 2.8 billion people live in areas where the demand for water is greater than the supply of clean water. This is a serious problem for all of us. We must find global solutions to protect people and businesses.

U.S. Government
Conflicts in other parts of the world could get worse because of water issues. One place where this could happen is Central and East Asia. The leaders there need to take steps to improve water management. It is in their self-interest to cooperate.

Historians
If so, it will surprise people. The only case of a war fought over water was more than 4,500 years ago in the Mideast. That is when two groups of people who lived in the areas between and around the Tigris and Euphrates Rivers went to war over the water supply.

| For | Supportive | Undecided | Unsupportive | Against |

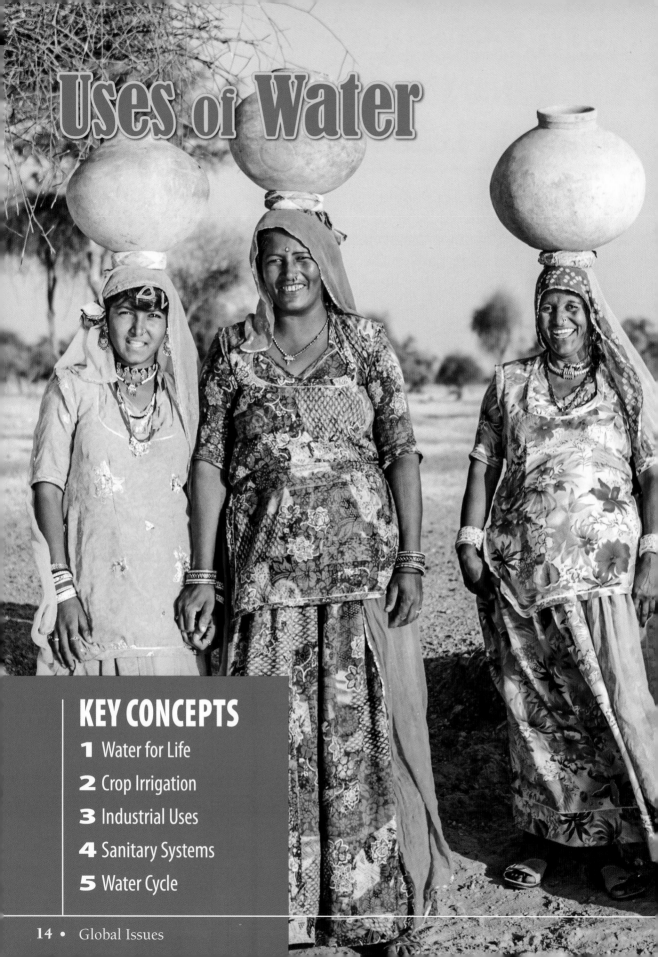

Uses of Water

Water managers need to consider all the uses of water and then decide how to distribute it. Water plays a key role in agriculture and industry. The lives of people, animals, and plants depend on it.

1 Water for Life

The Institute of Medicine states the average adult man should drink about 125 ounces (3.7 L) of liquids each day, while women should drink about 91 ounces (2.7 L). This also includes liquids consumed through food, which make up about 25 percent of daily liquid intake. Liquids flush out organs to clean them. Water also carries **nutrients** to the cells of the body and helps convert food into energy.

The human body is about 60 percent water by weight. Water is needed for the proper working of body systems, including breathing and blood circulation. People can go for more than a month without food, but they cannot survive without water for much longer than one week.

Since water is critical for life, keeping fresh water clean is a high priority. In developing countries, dirty, unsafe water kills more people each year than wars or other forms of violence. Children are most at risk. They have not developed resistance to the germs that can be found in dirty water.

Even in developed countries, the water supply must be protected from harmful substances. Sometimes, wastewater crosses into the water supply, bringing parasites, bacteria, and viruses. Also, chemicals that have not been disposed of properly can cross into the water supply. This can harm anyone who drinks from it.

In developed countries, officials continually test the water supply to make certain that the water is safe to drink. Standards have been set on the amounts of substances that are allowed in water systems. For example, limits are set on lead and copper. These substances can enter the water from plumbing pipes. A very small amount of lead or copper is not a danger. Too much of either, however, can lead to brain damage.

Every day, more and more lives depend on a decreasing supply of clean water. In the past 100 years, the world population has more than tripled. At the same time, water consumption is six times what it was 100 years ago. All of the plants and animals on Earth need fresh water, too.

> The human body is about 60 percent water by weight.

2 Crop Irrigation

Crops consume most of the world's available fresh water, so water managers study and try to improve methods of irrigation. Irrigation is the practice of moving water across land from a river, lake, or storage area such as a **reservoir**. Irrigation is needed to grow crops in areas that receive too little rainfall.

This practice is key to the food supply. The ability to move water allows farmers to grow much more food than would be possible otherwise. Worldwide, 670 million acres (270 million hectares) of farmland are irrigated. Irrigated farms in Asia account for 70 percent of the total land being used for agriculture.

For thousands of years, farmers have been irrigating their crops. Yet, the amount of irrigated land has doubled since 1960. This increase in irrigation has increased food production, but there is an ongoing demand for even more food. Today, the growth in population is greater than the growth in the use of irrigated land.

Improvements in irrigation would reduce waste and make an important difference in relieving the strain on the supply of fresh water. Groundwater is often used to irrigate farms. In some parts of the world, farmers have drained the groundwater down to dangerous levels. This has created deserts in areas that were once simply dry.

Main Types of Irrigation

DESCRIPTION AND DETAILS	PERCENTAGE OF WATER USED (NOT WASTED)
Surface (flowing water across ground)—used in more than 80 percent of irrigation worldwide	
Furrow method: involves running water into ruts along the ground; is cheap but requires a great deal of labor; negatives also include high water losses, wearing away of soil, and salt accumulation	20–60%
Basin method: involves building a wall around crops and flooding the middle; is cheap to install but requires a great deal of water; negatives also include salt accumulation and waterlogging	50–75%
Aerial (using sprinklers)—used in 10–15 percent of irrigation worldwide	
Costly to install and run; low pressure sprinklers easier to use	60–80%
Subsurface ("drip")—used in 1 percent of irrigation worldwide	
Method involves pipes and tubes that carry water to the plants' roots; is expensive and requires monitoring; is very efficient	75–95%

Do the Needs of Farmers Deserve Special Attention?

In 2007, a judge in California ordered the pumping stations in the Sacramento River **Delta** to reduce the amount of water delivered to the San Joaquin Valley. This valley is an area where many people live and where farmers grow many crops. The order was made because a kind of fish, called the delta smelt, was dying out.

The pumping plants in the delta were pulling in and grinding up the fish in the water. Delta smelt are rare and are protected by law. The judge's order helped to save the fish, but it cut down on the water supplied to California's Westlands Water District—the largest group of people sharing an irrigation system in the world. This caused problems for farmers in the area.

Farmers
We were hurt by the judge's order in California. The order was followed by a **drought**, so there was not enough water to keep our fields planted. Many of us suffered serious losses,and food production decreased.

Area Residents
The needs of our farmers must be taken seriously. They grow food people need and help the area economy. We want to protect fish and other animals, but water for our farmers is more important than one kind of fish.

Water Conservation Groups
Environmental issues such as the case in California force people to think about the water supply. We need to come up with better options. Farmers need water, but there may be other ways for them to get it.

Environmentalists
The water supply affects everyone, not just farmers. In California, for example, the Sacramento Delta and other areas are running out of water. The crisis caused by the court order was going to occur at some point anyway.

For   Supportive   Undecided   Unsupportive   Against

3 Industrial Uses

Industry is the second biggest user of water after farming. Farmers have been irrigating crops for many centuries. By contrast, industry is a relatively new development.

The **Industrial Revolution** began in Great Britain in the 1700s. Modernization spread throughout Europe and North America in the 1800s, and many people moved from rural to urban areas to work in factories. More recently, there has been a technological revolution. Rapid advancements in the use of computers have changed the way that industrial processes are carried out.

Most industrial use of water is efficient. Not much water is required, or care is taken so that the water is not wasted. Certain industrial processes, however, require vast amounts of water. Paper production, for example, requires a great deal of water. Newer methods of paper production use less water than older ones, but the paper industry still wastes a great deal of water.

Efforts are going on in some countries to reduce water use in industry. Increases in the price of water have helped to limit the waste of water. So have recycling and the use of new technologies. In the United States, industry today produces four times more than it did in 1950, and it uses only one-third the amount of water it used then. Japan and Germany show similar improvements in water use. In addition, Japanese industry recycles more than 75 percent of the water used to manufacture goods.

The greater challenge is in developing countries, where industrial water use is increasing sharply. In many of the world's developing countries, fresh water is scarce and the population is growing quickly. Their water supply systems are under growing strain.

Paper mills are usually built near large bodies of water because the mills need a great deal of water to operate.

4 Sanitary Systems

Huge quantities of water are used in sewage systems. A typical toilet in Europe flushes away more water in a day than an African family uses in a week. Recent laws in the United States and Japan require that new toilets have 1.3-gallon (5 L) "low-flush" systems. Older toilet tanks use twice as much water.

Traditionally, wastewater from sewage pipes, storm drains, and factories was discharged into rivers or the sea. Today, people recognize the pollution and health risks of discharging unclean water. The modern approach also views wastewater as a resource that can be put to valuable use. Wastewater that is carefully treated can be used in irrigation. It can also be used for drinking, bathing, and food preparation.

For example, Israel has spent a significant amount of money on wastewater treatment. Israel treats more than 90 percent of its wastewater, and treated wastewater accounts for most of the water used for irrigation in this desert nation. In the United States, a few cities, such as St. Petersburg, Florida, are successfully recycling their municipal wastewater back into the water systems tied to people's homes.

One way to reduce water use associated with sanitary systems is to prevent leaks. In many cities of the developing world, more than half of the water entering the system is lost through broken or leaking pipes and dripping taps. Repairing these problems would save much water.

Percentages of Global Water Use

Water is mainly used for irrigation, industry, and domestic, or household, requirements.

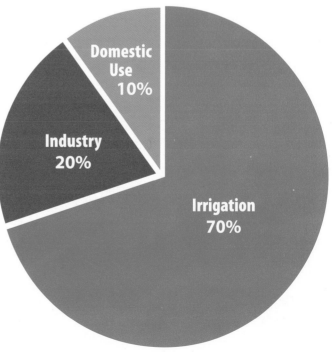

Domestic Use 10%
Industry 20%
Irrigation 70%

5 Water Cycle

Water is constantly used and reused by the water cycle. Understanding the water cycle is key to finding ways to conserve water. In the water cycle, fresh water falls as rain, snow, or hail. Some of this water evaporates, and water vapor rises into the air. Water also evaporates from plants in the process of **transpiration**. The vapor from both sources condenses into clouds.

In time, the clouds release water as precipitation, and it reaches the land. It then flows toward the sea in rivers or soaks into the soil as groundwater. Groundwater also flows toward the sea, unless it becomes trapped in rocks or aquifers. Usually, most of the water that reaches the ground flows downhill as runoff. The amount of runoff depends on the type of soil, the elevation or height of the ground, the slope of the land, and the vegetation. Runoff from cultivated land often carries substances that can lessen the water quality.

The amount of runoff varies from continent to continent. Asia has 30 percent of the world's runoff, while Africa has only 10 percent. Runoff flows downward due to gravity, as do rivers. This means that some nations benefit more from the water cycle just because of where they are located.

For example, 10 countries share the river basins of the Blue Nile and the White Nile in Africa. Egypt is the farthest downstream. Under the Nile Water Treaty of 1959, Egypt gets most of the water from these rivers. Conflicts occur whenever one of the countries located upstream wants to build a dam or construct an irrigation project on the Nile.

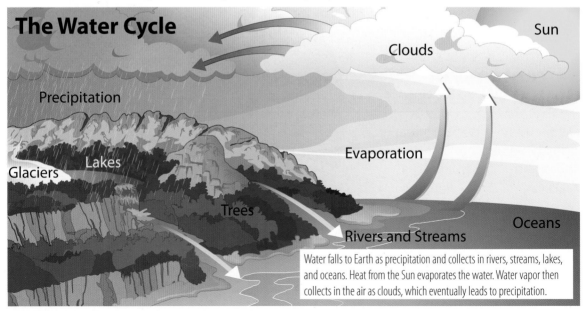

The Water Cycle

Sun

Clouds

Precipitation

Evaporation

Glaciers

Lakes

Trees

Oceans

Rivers and Streams

Water falls to Earth as precipitation and collects in rivers, streams, lakes, and oceans. Heat from the Sun evaporates the water. Water vapor then collects in the air as clouds, which eventually leads to precipitation.

Should Nations Try to Make Fresh Water from Saltwater?

With all the water in the oceans, it makes sense to try to figure out a way to use it. Many industries in the Middle East and California already use desalinated water. This is seawater that has had the salt removed. Some countries, such as Saudi Arabia, have invested large amounts of money in desalination plants to take the salt out of seawater.

The desalination process requires a large amount of energy and is very expensive. It also produces leftover salt and other chemicals. The desalination plants are left with the problem of what to do with the salt that has been removed from the water. The chemicals produced also can pollute coastal waters.

Nations Doing Desalination
Yes. Most of the water on Earth is seawater. It makes sense to convert it into something drinkable. The oceans are a secure source of water that can provide the water we need for years to come.

Equipment Manufacturers
Desalination is a good idea. Our equipment can help the nations around the world meet their water needs. The process does not create much pollution, beyond the salt that is left over. Steps can be taken to reduce this pollution.

Water Engineers
The process of removing salt from seawater provides limited amounts of water for drinking and irrigation. It should be done as part of a larger plan. Recycling water provides more usable fresh water than desalination does.

World Water Groups
Desalination is receiving increasing attention, but the process is far too expensive to be effective on a global scale. We need to approach the water supply problem from many sides. The solution begins with conservation.

For   Supportive   Undecided   Unsupportive   Against

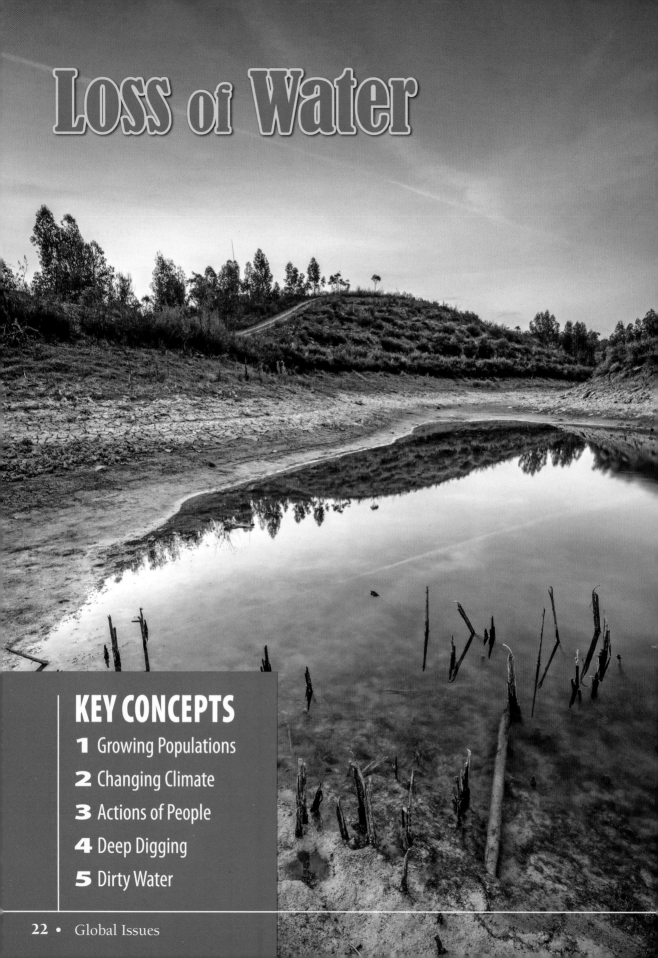

Loss of Water

KEY CONCEPTS

1 Growing Populations

2 Changing Climate

3 Actions of People

4 Deep Digging

5 Dirty Water

At the end of 2012, the population of the world reached 7 billion. According to population studies, there may be 9 billion people on Earth by the year 2070. All of these people need water, but there may not be enough.

1 Growing Populations

Across the globe, cities are growing, and more people are living modern lifestyles. According to the World Resources Institute, the use of water has been increasing at twice the rate of the increase in population. When people have a higher standard of living, they use more water.

By 2025, water use is expected to increase by 50 percent in developing countries. In developed countries, water use is likely to increase by 18 percent. Already, the demand for water has been greater than the supply in parts of China, Russia, and the southern United States.

Over the past decade, the freshwater reserves throughout much of the Middle East have shrunk by 35 cubic miles (144 cubic kilometers). This is about one-third the volume of Lake Erie. The number of people in the Middle East is expected to grow by more than 50 percent by 2025. This means the water supply strain will be even greater in that part of the world.

How might this affect the people of the Middle East? Farms may be forced out of business. There may be too little drinking water. More food may have to be imported because there is not enough water to support farming in those countries.

Most likely, international cooperation will be needed to solve the problem and avoid a crisis. The Challenge Program on Water and Food, which is a worldwide group involved with such issues, studied the water supplies of a number of countries. The group found that food production could be doubled in parts of Africa, Asia, and Latin America if all the people living along the length of a river or near another water source would cooperate with one another.

In the West Bank, between Israel and Jordan, canals carry water to crops on land that would otherwise be barren.

Mapping Water Resources

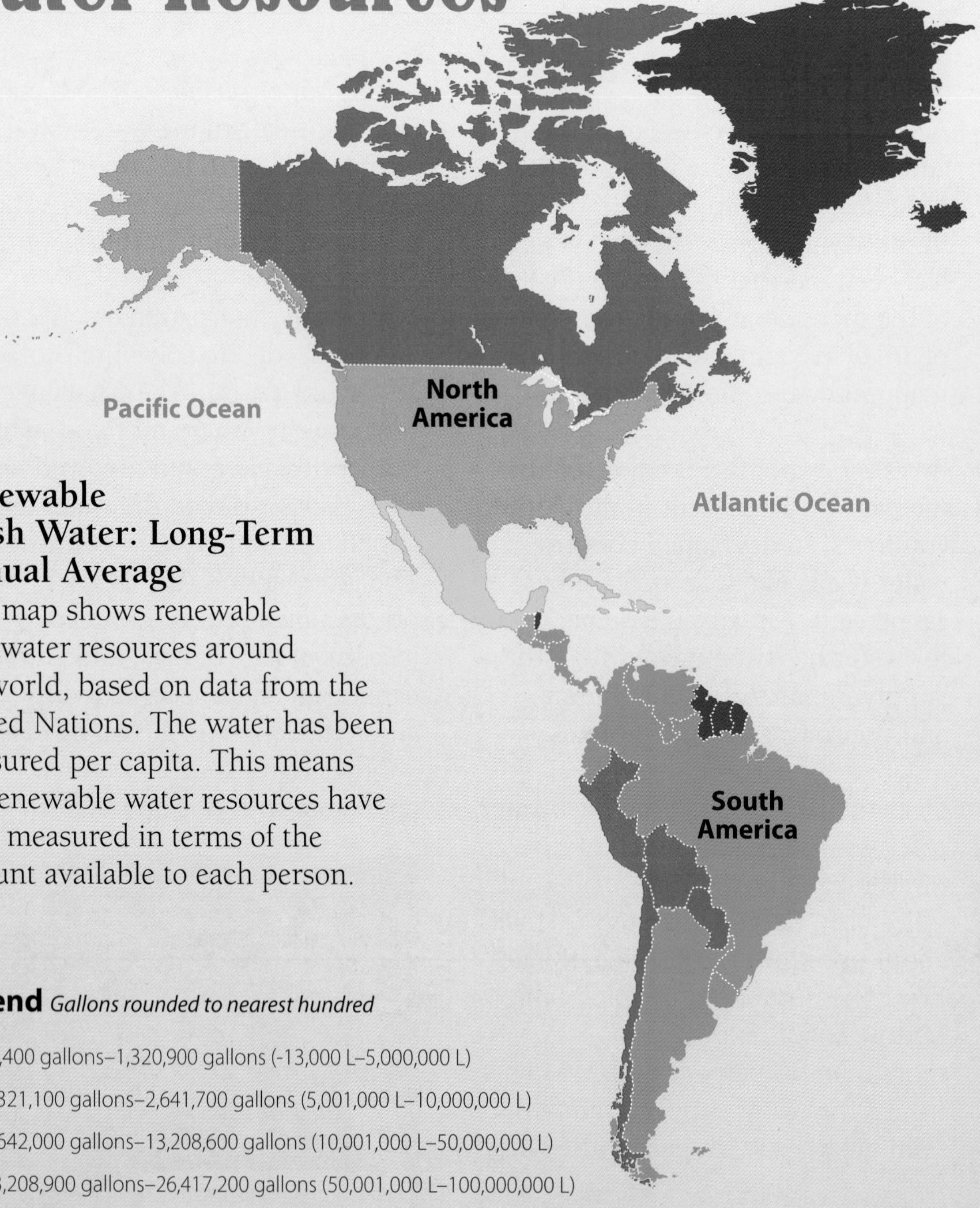

Pacific Ocean

North America

Atlantic Ocean

South America

Renewable Fresh Water: Long-Term Annual Average

This map shows renewable freshwater resources around the world, based on data from the United Nations. The water has been measured per capita. This means the renewable water resources have been measured in terms of the amount available to each person.

Legend *Gallons rounded to nearest hundred*

- ☐ -3,400 gallons–1,320,900 gallons (-13,000 L–5,000,000 L)
- ☐ 1,321,100 gallons–2,641,700 gallons (5,001,000 L–10,000,000 L)
- ☐ 2,642,000 gallons–13,208,600 gallons (10,001,000 L–50,000,000 L)
- ☐ 13,208,900 gallons–26,417,200 gallons (50,001,000 L–100,000,000 L)
- ☐ 26,417,500 gallons–2,787,015,200 gallons (100,001,000 L–10,550,000,000 L)
- ☐ No Data

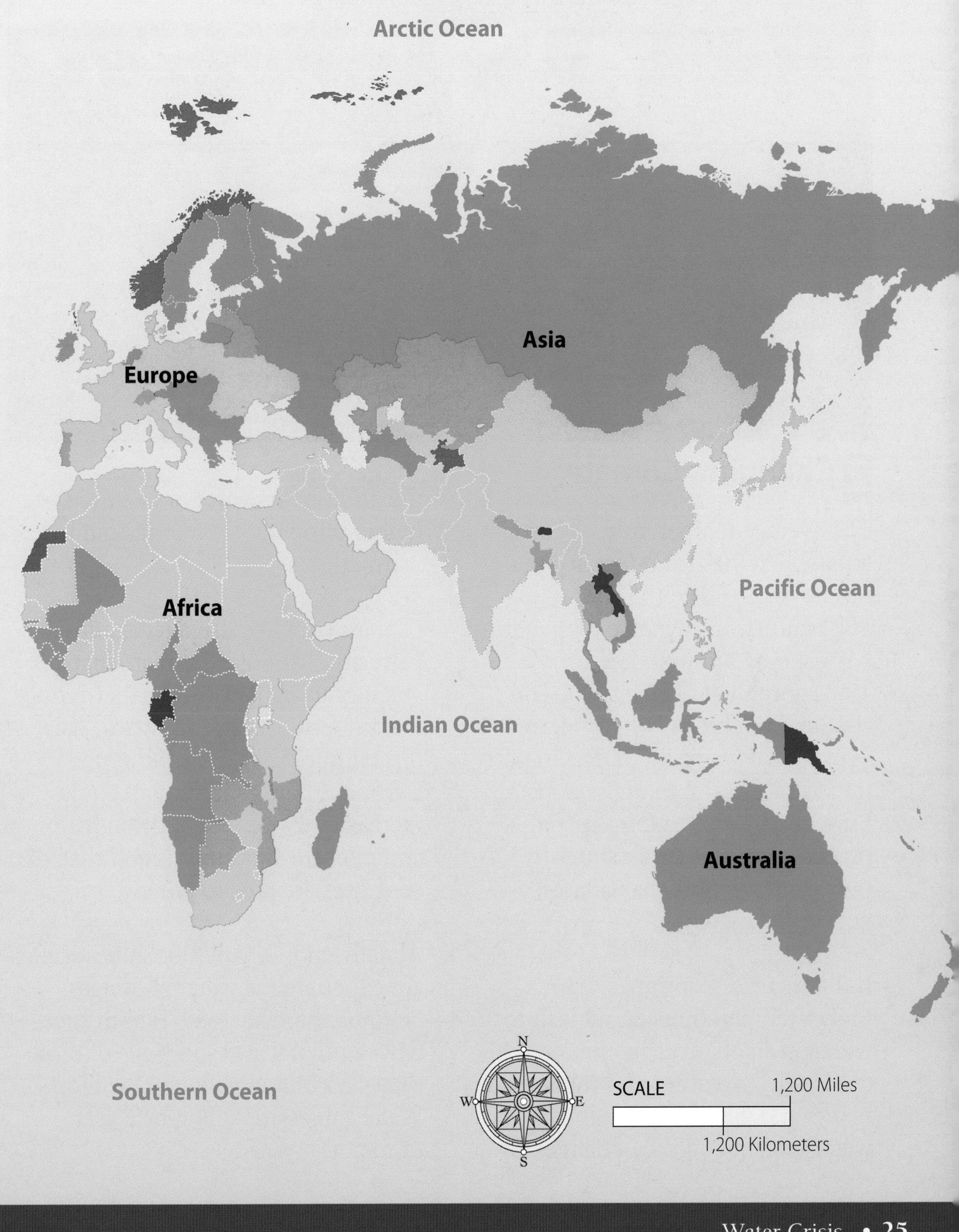

Arctic Ocean

Asia

Europe

Pacific Ocean

Africa

Indian Ocean

Australia

Southern Ocean

N
W   E
S

SCALE

1,200 Miles

1,200 Kilometers

A recent drought in China caused water shortages for more than a half million people in the province of Hubel, where many crops dried up and died.

2 Changing Climate

The average temperature of Earth's atmosphere has been increasing in recent years. Since the start of the 20th century, the average temperature has risen by approximately 1.4° Fahrenheit (1° Celsius). This rise in temperature, often referred to as global warming, is due in part to natural causes. Many scientists, however, believe that industrial processes and other activities by the world's people play a large part in the increase.

If the increase continues, the higher temperatures could lead to widespread changes in climate. This could affect weather and the lives of plants and animals. All parts of the water system could be changed by the additional heat. For example, higher temperatures could lead to warmer seas.

Global warming also affects rainfall patterns. Scientists estimate that changes in rainfall will further reduce the amount of water in Africa, Asia, the Middle East, and southern Europe. Changes in rainfall could increase the number of droughts and alter the amount of food that countries are able to grow.

Already, more than 400 Chinese cities are experiencing water shortages. Beijing, Shanghai, and Tianjin each have annual water shortfalls of more than 525 billion gallons (2 trillion L). Water tables are falling by 3 feet (1 meter) a year.

Should Countries Ship Water to Other Nations?

Canada is rich in fresh water. Yet nearby, in the United States, many places are experiencing water shortages. Politicians and businesspeople have been considering plans to ship water from Canada to dry places in the United States and elsewhere.

More than a decade ago, various Canadian businesspeople offered plans to export water to other nations. One man planned to drain water from a lake in Newfoundland and send it through pipes to ships in a harbor. Officials in the Canadian government, however, banned most kinds of large-scale water removal. Today, only the sale of bottled water is allowed, but as water shortages increase, Canada and other water-rich nations may rethink their options.

Businesspeople
Lack of water is often a temporary problem that arises after a drought. Countries do not need to spend money on costly dams or desalination projects. We can ship water to them as needed—and make money while doing it.

Shipping Companies
It is expensive to ship water in bulk. It is much easier and less costly to ship bottled water. However, if we find that there are countries that want us to ship water in bulk and are willing to pay for it, we will find a way to do so.

Governments in Countries Needing Water
It would be helpful to receive needed water, but we are not set up to receive large shipments. There are not enough loading facilities. For now, it is better to think about desalination and other solutions.

Governments in Countries with Water
Even though we have water, this is not a good idea. We need to think in the long term and in the best interests of our own people. Water should not be treated as a good to be traded. It is a resource that needs to be managed.

For   Supportive   Undecided   Unsupportive   Against

3 Actions of People

Large building projects can cause changes that can hurt the water cycle. When land is covered with plants, it acts as a sponge that absorbs rainfall. Removal of the plants allows rainfall to run off the surface of the land. Then, the soil begins to wear away. For example, when forests were cleared to build India's Kabini Dam project, the amount of rainfall the region's land absorbed decreased. A similar reduction in rainfall collection has taken place in other parts of the world after large-scale forest clearance.

In the past 100 years, when people have been faced with major water shortages, they have often changed the face of Earth to try to solve the problem. They have built dams, changed the courses of rivers, built canals, or invested in other major projects to manage water. More than 40,000 large dams have been built worldwide. Dams control the flow of water, which reduces the risk of floods. Dams also harness the water for irrigation or **power generation**. Large dams, however, can have a negative effect on the environment, as well as on the people living near them.

Fewer big dams are being built today, but people are still feeling the effects of dams that have already been built. In the 1950s, the Soviet Union changed the course of the Amu Darya and the Syr Darya rivers. These rivers once flowed into the Aral Sea, which was once the fourth-largest inland body of water in the world. It is now one-quarter of its former size, and it is still shrinking.

Before the Aral Sea shrank, the area's fishing industry supplied 50,000 tons (45,000 tonnes) of freshwater fish per year. This industry supported 60,000 jobs. Now, there is no fishing industry on the Aral. In addition, the wind blows salty, toxic dust off the dry seabed. This endangers the health of thousands of people throughout the region.

The Aral Sea of Central Asia began to dry up in the 1930s, when many more irrigation canals began tapping into it.

Turkey is undergoing a dramatic decline in water levels. Crops are drying in areas where an enormous lake once stood.

4 Deep Digging

In the quest for water, people have changed water sources located beneath the ground. Many farmers use power-driven wells to raise underground water for irrigation. As a result, water tables have been dropping. Groundwater levels are falling on every continent.

In Asia, rice is a major food source. Growing rice requires a large amount of water. This adds to problems of water scarcity in places such as China, India, and Pakistan. The aquifers in Asia have been used for thousands of years. The water level in some aquifers has dropped so low that it is now difficult to irrigate crops in areas that rely on their underground water supplies.

The United States is facing similar issues. Important farming states, such as Kansas and Texas, are having problems. The land that can be irrigated is shrinking as the groundwater is used up.

The most serious problems in the United States are in the dry Southwest, including Arizona and New Mexico. Pumps and wells have removed much of the groundwater in these areas. In the Southwest, there is very little rain each year. The aquifers cannot refill fast enough, and the water tables continue to lower.

5 Dirty Water

The developed world has been struggling to clean up pollution in rivers and lakes. Meanwhile, in the developing world, sewage and industrial waste are being poured into some rivers at an alarming rate. About 95 percent of sewage in developing countries is released into rivers without treatment of any kind.

Cleaning up polluted water is a major issue, especially when underground water is involved. Flowing water can clean itself of **pollutants**, but underground aquifers do not flow. It is both difficult and expensive to clean this water. The process can take many years. A flowing river can renew itself in two or three weeks, but an aquifer may take hundreds or even thousands of years.

Water **contamination** results in nearly 30,000 human deaths per week worldwide. Arsenic, cadmium, copper, lead, and mercury are some of the more common contaminants found in rivers and lakes around the world. Before such water can be used safely, it has to undergo a costly treatment process.

Dirty water must be cleaned even for industrial processes. Water **purification** plants remove bacteria and chemicals from the water. Some purification plants can even reclaim wastewater from the sewers. They clean and recycle the water back to consumers as usable water.

The polluted water is often treated with chemicals. Chlorine and iodine are commonly used for this process. Filtration is an effective method of water purification, too. In this method, a filter separates solid material from the water. Filtration can be used with chemical treatment.

Threats to Groundwater

Threats to groundwater include the pesticides used on lawns and farms and the chemicals released in industrial processes.

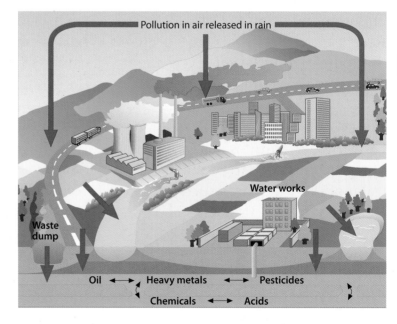

Pollution in air released in rain

Waste dump

Water works

Oil ↔ Heavy metals ↔ Pesticides

Chemicals ↔ Acids

Should Developed Nations Share Their Water Technology?

Clean water is a fairly modern development. The United States did not have widespread laws regarding clean water until the 1940s. After clean water became common, many diseases were nearly wiped out in developed countries. The general health of their populations improved.

Today, billions of people worldwide still do not have clean drinking water. They need basic sanitation. Technology exists to provide these basics to every person on Earth. Should nations with that technology be required to share it with other nations?

Global-Minded Activists	Military Strategists	Budget-Minded Conservationists	Those Who Believe in "Country First"
Yes, people should make an effort to share what they have and know. Water management must benefit everyone, in both developed and developing nations. We must share technology and use it to solve the water crisis.	Dirty water is a threat to people's health and to the security of nations. People might go to war to get clean water. We need to take steps to see that everyone has clean water, which includes sharing the related technology.	All nations depend on the same pool of resources. Education is needed most, not expensive technology. With education, everyone learns to conserve water.	No, it is not the responsibility of any country to help any other country with its natural resources. We should concentrate on taking care of our own people and problems first. Meddling with others just leads to trouble.

| For | Supportive | Undecided | Unsupportive | Against |

Protection of Water

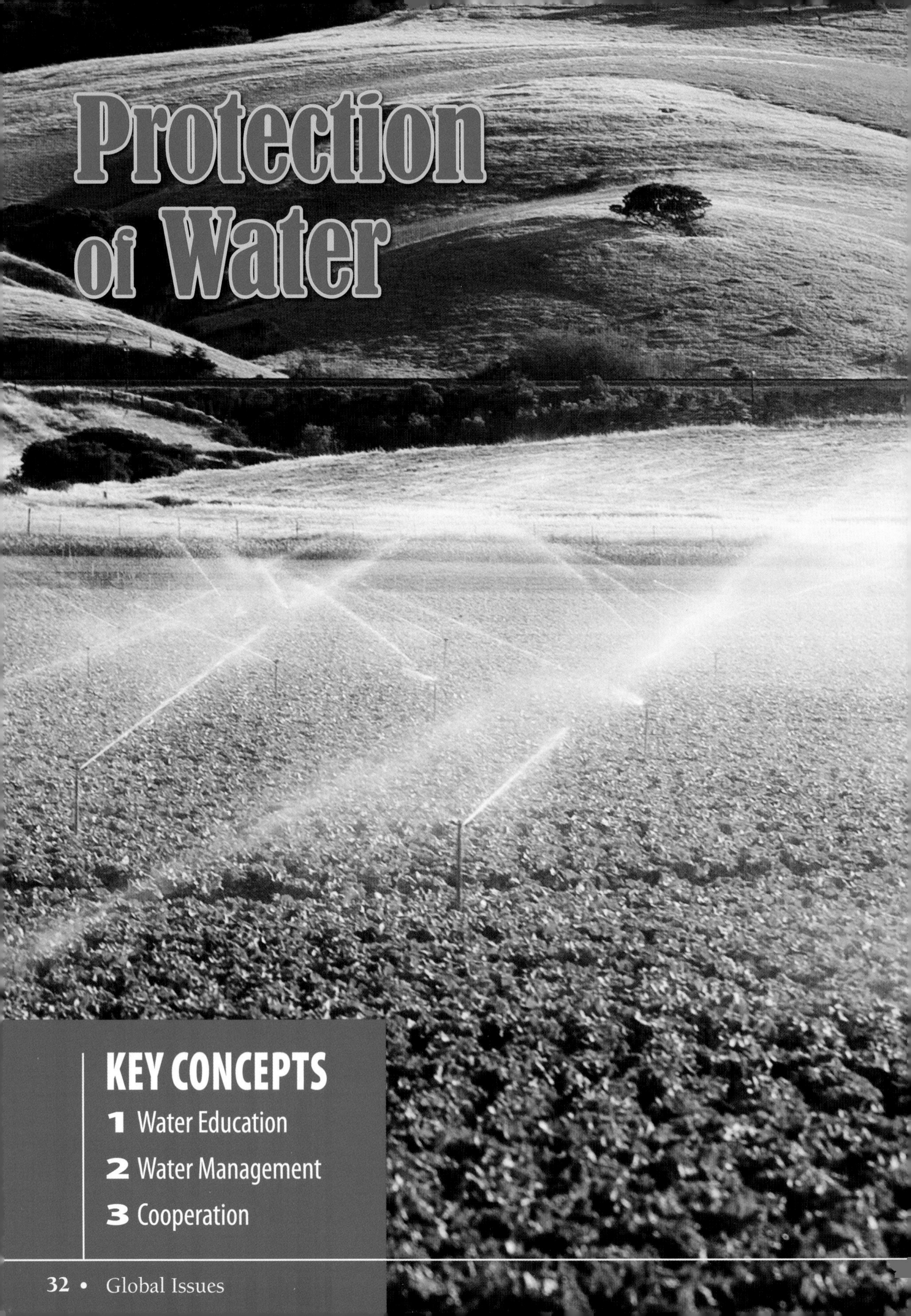

KEY CONCEPTS

1 Water Education

2 Water Management

3 Cooperation

The solution to the world's water crisis begins with education. Education can help people understand that water is a precious resource. With education, everyone can make better decisions about water projects and learn to conserve and build upon the supply of fresh water.

1 Water Education

One way that officials are teaching people is to charge more money for water. For example, Southern California is a desert region where very little water occurs naturally. Yet, the area is filled with golf courses, gardens, swimming pools, and farms because a large amount of water is piped in. Consumers there pay high fees for their water and lifestyles.

To better manage the water supply, officials are studying the lessons of the past. Big projects that change rivers are not always the answer. For example, when the Erie Canal was built in New York State in the 1800s, a creature called the sea lamprey was introduced to the Great Lakes. The sea lamprey killed most of the salmon in the Great Lakes and ruined the fishing industry there.

Business officials have been learning lessons from the past as well. The Rhine River flows through much of Europe. Many power plants and other structures were built there. Businesses dumped chemicals and other waste into the water. In recent years, expensive efforts have been made to clean the Rhine.

2 Water Management

Dams control flooding and provide **hydroelectric power**. They benefit the people in the affected regions. Officials now know, though, that there may also be huge costs.

China's Three Gorges Dam was completed in 2006. The dam diverts water from the Yangtze River to the North China Plain and is the world's largest source of hydroelectric power. The Three Gorges Dam has prevented flooding in some areas but has also been blamed for causing serious problems. For example, it has weakened riverbanks, leading to landslides.

Going forward, water management projects must be carefully planned. Ideally, dams are built where there are large amounts of precipitation, where steep hills catch the water quickly, and where the soil is hard enough so that water does not soak into the ground too fast. Reservoirs need to be carefully placed so the water is not wasted through evaporation. Evaporation is not as big a problem in hilly areas. Still, some evaporation from the surface of the collected water does occur.

3 Cooperation

Sometimes, governments find themselves in conflict over a limited supply of water. For example, there is very little water in the Middle East. Middle Eastern countries often compete for the same water supply. These countries also often find themselves in conflict over oil, land, and religion.

Syria and Iraq rely on water from the Tigris and Euphrates rivers, which begin in Turkey. In 1990, Turkey built a new dam and blocked the Euphrates so that a reservoir behind the dam could be filled. For a time, the water supply in Syria and Iraq slowed to a trickle. This caused friction between the nations. Recently, the three nations have held talks about sharing their water sources. The relationships between these nations are still difficult, but they know they face the same water problem together.

Water shortages do not have to lead to conflict. The need to share water resources can also lead to understanding and cooperation among nations. More than 500 million people live in the valleys of the Indus, Ganges, and Brahmaputra rivers in Asia. This is the largest irrigation network in the world. The people of India, Pakistan, and Bangladesh have conflicts on many issues. Despite their difficult relationships, they have managed to work out complex water-sharing agreements.

Water shortages, contamination, and conflicts have been occurring for thousands of years. Now, these issues have reached a point of crisis. As countries further develop, they must do so with the knowledge that water is Earth's most precious resource. It must be respected, conserved, and used wisely.

Local water sources are a part of the global water supply. The World Health Organization is encouraging people to conserve and protect their water sources as a direct and daily way to contribute to a better world.

Should People Eat Vegetarian Diets as a Way to Conserve Water?

Even diet has an impact on the water supply. The production of 1 ton (0.9 tonnes) of chicken meat takes twice as much water as raising 1 ton (0.9 tonnes) of rice. Beef production uses 10 times as much water as rice production. In general terms, the trend in the developing world toward eating more meat is a sign of economic improvement because meat is expensive. However, the increased demand for meat puts an extra strain on water resources. Some people have suggested that encouraging people to eat vegetarian diets is an easy way to conserve water.

Vegetarians
Yes. It takes at least three times as much water to feed a meat-eater as it does to feed a vegetarian. Water is needed to grow grain to feed the animals and to give the animals water to drink. Being a vegetarian is a good way to save water.

Environmentalists
In addition to using a great deal of water, livestock are a major source of water pollution. Animal wastes pollute groundwater and streams. Less demand for animals would lead to less pollution, so people should eat less meat.

Meat Eaters
Eating meat provides important nutrients needed by the human brain and body systems. History shows that human beings developed by eating meat, not just plants. There must be other ways for us to conserve water.

Ranchers
Targeting meat is not the answer. If you want to save water, cut down on the other kinds of foods you waste, because that would cut down on the demand for crops. More water is wasted on irrigation than anything else.

For   Supportive   Undecided   Unsupportive   Against

Water through History

Throughout history, humans have searched for and protected safe water supplies. The first civilizations grew up around the major rivers of the world. By 7000 BC, irrigation was in use along the Nile Valley in Egypt. Improvements in water technology allowed people to flourish across the globe.

6000 BC
Irrigation is widespread in the fertile delta between the Tigris and Euphrates rivers in the Mideast.

4000 BC
Susa, a city in Iran, pioneers the use of toilets with drainage.

605–562 BC
Residents of Babylon get running water.

400 BC
China is building the first sections of the Grand Canal, which will eventually connect more than 1,700 miles (2,700 kilometers) of waterways.

100 BC– AD 400
In the Roman Empire, aqueducts carry water to cities and towns. The water is used for drinking, bathing, and sanitation.

1400

80
Rome passes a law to protect water stored during dry periods.

1400
The spread of force pumps, or water wheels, changes the way water is transported. River currents power huge wheels that pump water to reservoirs.

100 BC

1901

The first Federal Water Power Act becomes law in the United States, beginning a period of building large hydroelectric plants.

1908

The chemical chlorine is used to purify water in a New Jersey reservoir. This is the first public water supply in the United States to be treated this way in an effort to remove impurities and contaminants.

1948

Frank Zybach invents the center-pivot irrigation machine, which spreads water in a circle. This development is a revolution in irrigation technology.

1974

The Safe Drinking Water Act is passed in the United States, authorizing the Environmental Protection Agency to set health-based standards for water.

1992

The United Nations promotes the idea of a World Water Day, to be recognized each year on March 22.

2001

The theme for World Water Day is "Water for Health—Taking Charge." The World Health Organization leads the campaign. Each year, the UN highlights a different aspect of fresh water for World Water Day. To promote cooperation, the UN asks different agencies to take charge of the program.

2013

A University of Florida study looks at data for 225 U.S. cities. The study finds that 17 percent of people living in urban areas now face moderate to severe risk of water shortages in their areas.

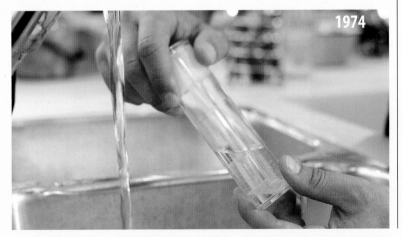

Working in Water Management

AQUATIC ECOLOGIST

Duties Studying water **ecosystems** and advising public or private organizations about water management strategies

Education A bachelor's degree in science

Interest The relationship between living things and the water around them

Aquatic ecologists study the relationship between living things and their water environment. This work involves research on water systems. The day-to-day duties are a mix of doing field research, conducting experiments, and writing reports. Aquatic ecologists often travel to a body of water to collect samples of its plants and animals for study. Later, the ecologists present a report on their findings. Most aquatic ecologists have a science degree. Senior ecologists usually have a master's degree or a doctoral degree. Many begin their careers as research assistants in a university or college. Then, they may take a position with a government agency or an environmental organization.

HYDRAULICS ENGINEER

Duties Designing dams and supervising construction

Education A bachelor's degree in civil engineering or similar

Interest Construction, math, drawing, and physics

Hydraulics engineers design dams. They need to have strong math, science, and computer skills. They must also be familiar with building materials, environmental issues, and safety regulations. In addition, they must be skilled communicators. Most of the time, hydraulics engineers work in an office, where they use computer-aided design, or CAD, systems to develop plans. At times, they visit job sites. This job may require travel to isolated areas, walking long distances, working in tight spaces, and climbing to tall heights.

HYDROLOGIST

Duties Analyzing information about water resources

Education A bachelor's degree in science

Interest Water resource management

Hydrologists study watersheds, which are areas drained by more than one water system. Typically, their time is divided between lab work and fieldwork. Hydrologists often collect water samples, which they then inspect in a laboratory to determine water quality. If the water quality is low, the hydrologist makes recommendations about improving it. Day-to-day duties can also include managing staff, developing budgets, and designing programs to develop or protect a watershed. This job requires a degree in geology or a related environmental subject.

IRRIGATION TECHNOLOGIST

Duties Designing systems for sustainable irrigation and studying their use

Education A diploma in irrigation technology or a degree in agricultural science or engineering

Interest Efficient water delivery systems

Irrigation technologists are in charge of developing systems for the distribution of water. Some specialize in irrigation for farms, while others may be experts in irrigation for cities, which is often called urban industrial irrigation. In each case, irrigation technologists work toward sustainable irrigation plans and practices. Technologists examine maps, photographs taken from airplanes and satellites, and other data to determine the needs of an area. They use computer programs to design systems of pumps and pipelines. Some technologists have engineering degrees, while others have a background in agricultural or environmental science. Senior irrigation technologists often provide reports for corporations.

Key Water Protection Organizations

INTERNATIONAL WATER ACADEMY

Goal Fostering a community of water experts who can benefit humankind

Reach Worldwide

Facts Has a special interest in managing water conflicts

The International Water Academy seeks to develop water management practices and to encourage international cooperation. The group works in partnership with a variety of government, business, and private organizations. The International Water Academy provides educational services about the use and conservation of the world's water resources. It teaches the principles, trends, and technology of modern water management to people around the world. Its work includes water monitoring, research into water transport, and training in water conflict resolution. The Academy's motto is "Saving water, one drop at a time."

UN-WATER

Goal Safeguarding the health of the environment and especially the water supply

Reach Worldwide

Facts Formed in 2003 to unite various United Nations agencies concerned with water issues

UN-Water runs the World Water Assessment Programme, which studies water data from around the world. UN-Water works with the World Health Organization to monitor how well different nations are meeting their goals for clean water. One of its projects is the UN-Water Decade Programme on Advocacy and Communication. This teaches communities and groups how to reduce poverty through water management. UN-Water makes its maps, charts, and other information available to the public. Every three years, UN-Water publishes a report on the state of the world's freshwater resources, to help the world's leaders make important decisions.

USGS

Goal Scientific research on the health of U.S. ecosystems and the environment

Reach United States

Facts Has more than 400 locations throughout the United States

The U.S. Geological Survey (USGS) is an independent fact-finding agency. It investigates issues related to natural resources in the United States. Created by an act of Congress, the USGS has been in operation since 1879. There are about 10,000 scientists and other staff members. Among their tasks are collecting water samples and conducting experiments to manage water and other natural resources. The USGS conducts the National Water Quality Assessment Program. It is also active in the education of the public, including students, about water quality and other subjects related to the environment.

WATER AND SANITATION PROGRAM

Goal Sustaining water for all people in a changing climate

Reach Worldwide

Facts Within the last decade, the group has more than tripled the amount of money committed to water projects

The Water and Sanitation Program is run by the World Bank. The World Bank is one of the largest sources of funds for member nations. As part of its mission to raise living standards, the World Bank helps nations adapt to the world's changing climate and the change in water supplies. The Water and Sanitation Program has experts who study water management to share what they know. They examine the relationship between the environment, society, poverty, and health. The program helps people gain access to clean water and sanitation services through private and public programs. The program's overall goal is sustainable solutions for a global water supply.

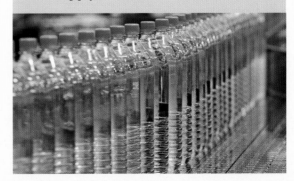

Research a Water Conservation Issue

The Issue

Conservation is a subject of much debate. Many groups may not agree on the best way to conserve water and keep water clean. It is important to enter into a discussion to hear all the points of view before making decisions. Discussing issues will make sure that the actions taken are beneficial for all involved.

Get The Facts

Choose an issue (Political, Cultural, Ecological, or Economic) from the book. Then, pick one of groups presented in the issue spectrum. Using the book and research in the library or on the Internet, find out more about the members of the group and their views on water conservation. What is important to them? Why are they backing or opposing the particular issue? What claims or facts can they use to support their point of view? Be sure to write clear and concise supporting arguments for your group. Focus on the environment and how the group's needs relate to it. Will this group be affected in a positive or negative way by changes in the environment around them?

Use the Concept Web

A concept web is a useful research tool. Read the information and review the structure in the concept web on the next page. Use the relationships between concepts to help you understand your group's point of view.

Organize Your Research

Sort your information into organized points. Make sure your research clearly answers what impact the issue will have on your chosen group, how that impact will affect them, and why they have chosen their

CONSERVATION CONCEPT WEB

Use this concept web to understand the network of factors contributing to the water crisis.

- Much of fresh water is polluted
- Dirty water carries diseases, such as giardiasis
- Wastewater needs treatment
- Leaks must be controlled

- Much fresh water is trapped in ice around poles
- Water cycle affects supply
- Monsoons and other weather events affect supply
- Aquifers store water underground and need protection
- Runoff also needs protections

- Crops are major consumer of fresh water
- Increased food production is still needed
- Too much irrigated water is wasted
- Systems need updating

Sanitation

Freshwater Resources

Irrigation

WATER CRISIS

Management

Cooperation

Technology

- Water tables are dropping
- Groundwater is not really renewable
- Desalination produces water from seawater
- Processes need improvements
- Various jobs in water management

- Some 40 percent of world is experiencing shortages
- Conflicts possible
- Water groups attempt to increase cooperation
- Cooperation needed by individuals as well

- Dams capture and direct water
- Pumping plants create electricity
- Negative effects from human interventions
- Broader, smarter plans are needed

Test Your Knowledge

Answer each of the questions below to test your knowledge of the water crisis issue.

1 What percentage of Earth is covered with water?

2 What is giardiasis?

3 What does an aquatic ecologist study?

4 Name a chemical that is used to clean water.

5 What percentage of a person's body weight is water?

6 Which nation has one-fifth of the world's fresh water?

7 Which continent has the most irrigated farms?

8 What is desalination?

9 Only one-fourth of the rivers and lakes in the United States have been damaged by pollution. True or false?

10 How many people in the world do not have clean water for drinking or bathing?

ANSWERS 1. 71 percent **2.** A water-borne disease caused by a parasite that lives in the intestines **3.** Water ecosystems **4.** Chlorine or iodine **5.** About 60 percent **6.** Canada **7.** Asia **8.** The process of taking the salt from seawater **9.** False **10.** About 780 million

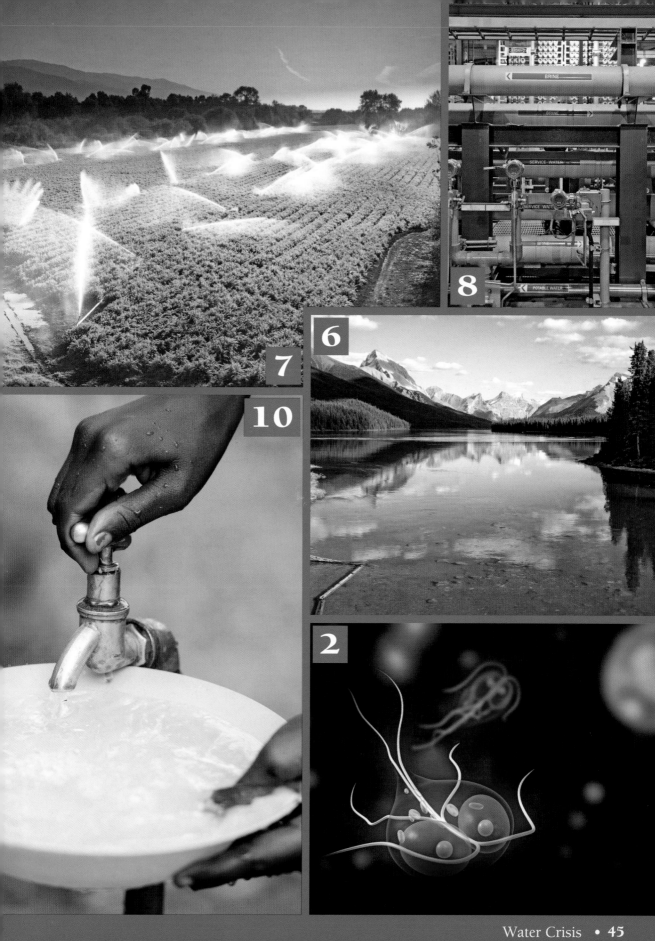

Key Words

aqueduct: a structure for carrying water over a long distance

contamination: the process of making something unclean or impure

dams: barriers that block water and control its flow, creating a reservoir

delta: a flat area at the mouth of some rivers, where the main stream splits into several streams

developed world: countries with high average incomes and advanced industries

developing world: countries with low average income that until recently had little manufacturing and technology

drought: a long period of little or no precipitation

ecosystems: communities of plants and animals interacting with their environment

extinct: no longer alive

fresh water: water that is not salty

groundwater: supplies of fresh water located below the surface of land

hydroelectric power: electric power produced by harnessing the energy of moving water

Industrial Revolution: a period in the 1700s and 1800s when machinery was developed to do many types of work and large factories became common for manufacturing

irrigation: a system for moving water so that crops can be grown

municipalities: political units formed for self-government, such as that of a town

nutrients: things needed by people, plants, and animals to live and grow

pipelines: lines of pipe with pumps, valves, and control devices for transporting liquids and gases

pollutants: toxins that contaminate air, water, or soil

power generation: creating electric power from other forms of energy

purification: to make free from pollutants

renewable: able to be replaced by natural processes

reservoir: a place where water is collected and stored for use

sanitation: conditions related to clean water and to waste disposal

standard of living: level of wealth and material comfort available to people

transpiration: passing of water through a plant from the roots to the air around the plant

United Nations (UN): organization that promotes international cooperation and includes most nations of the world

water tables: upper surfaces of groundwater where water fills all the holes of the soil

World Bank: an international organization that helps developing nations by providing money, advice, and research to aid their economic advancement

Index

Log on to www.av2books.com

AV² by Weigl brings you media enhanced books that support active learning. Go to www.av2books.com, and enter the special code found on page 2 of this book. You will gain access to enriched and enhanced content that supplements and complements this book. Content includes video, audio, weblinks, quizzes, a slide show, and activities.

AV² Online Navigation

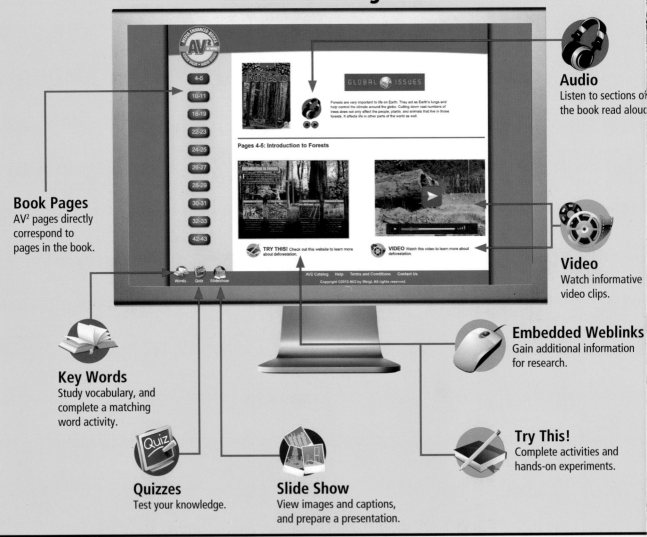

Book Pages
AV² pages directly correspond to pages in the book.

Audio
Listen to sections of the book read aloud

Video
Watch informative video clips.

Key Words
Study vocabulary, and complete a matching word activity.

Embedded Weblinks
Gain additional information for research.

Quizzes
Test your knowledge.

Slide Show
View images and captions, and prepare a presentation.

Try This!
Complete activities and hands-on experiments.

AV² was built to bridge the gap between print and digital. We encourage you to tell us what you like and what you want to see in the future.

Sign up to be an AV² Ambassador at www.av2books.com/ambassador.